The French Revolution

ERIC HOBSBAWM

A Phoenix Paperback

This abridged edition, published in 1996 by Phoenix,
contains chapter 3, pages 53 to 76 of
The Age of Revolution 1789–1848.

First published in 1975 by Weidenfeld & Nicolson
a division of Orion Books Ltd
Orion House, 5 Upper St Martin's Lane, London WC2H 9EA

ISBN 1 85799 531 7

Typeset by CentraCet Ltd, Cambridge
Printed in Great Britain by
Clays Ltd, St Ives plc

The French Revolution

An Englishman not filled with esteem and admiration at the sublime *manner in which one of the most* IMPORTANT REVOLUTIONS *the world has ever seen is now effecting, must be dead to every sense of virtue and of freedom; not one of my countrymen who has had the* good fortune *to witness the transactions of the last three days in this great city, but will testify that my language is not hyperbolical.*

The *Morning Post* (July 21, 1789) on the fall of the Bastille

Soon the enlightened nations will put on trial those who have hitherto ruled over them. The kings shall flee into the deserts, into the company of the wild beasts whom they resemble; and Nature shall resume her rights.

Saint-Just. *Sur la Constitution de la France, Discours prononcé à la Convention 24 avril* 1793

If the economy of the nineteenth century world was formed mainly under the influence of the British Industrial Revolution, its politics and ideology were formed mainly by the French. Britain provided the model for its railways and factories, the economic explosive which cracked open the traditional economic and social structures of the non-European world; but France made its revolutions and gave them their ideas, to the point where a tricolour of some kind became the emblem of virtually every emerging nation, and European (or indeed world) politics between 1789 and 1917 were largely the struggle for and against the principles of 1789, or the even more incendiary ones of 1793. France provided the vocabulary and the issues of liberal and radical-democratic politics for most of the world. France provided the first great example, the concept and the vocabulary of nationalism. France provided the codes of law, the model of scientific and technical organization, the metric system of measurement for most countries. The ideology of the modern world first penetrated the ancient civilizations which had hitherto resisted European ideas through French influence. This was the work of the French Revolution.*

The later eighteenth century was an age of crisis for the old régimes of Europe and their economic systems, and its last decades were filled with political agitations sometimes reaching the point of revolt, of colonial movements for autonomy sometimes reaching that of secession: not only in the USA (1776–83), but also in Ireland (1782–4), in Belgium and Liège (1787–90), in Holland (1783–7), in Geneva, even – it has been argued – in England (1779). So striking is this clustering of political unrest that some recent historians have spoken of an 'age of democratic revolution' of which the French was only one, though the most dramatic and far-reaching.[1]

---

* This difference between the British and French influences should not be pushed too far. Neither centre of the dual revolution confined its influence to any special field of human activity and the two were complementary rather than competitive. However, even when both converged most clearly – as in *socialism*, which was almost simultaneously invented and named in both countries – they converged from somewhat different directions.

1 See R. R. Palmer, *The Age of Democratic Revolution* (1959); J. Godechot, *La Grande Nation* (1956), Vol. I, Chapter 1.

Insofar as the crisis of the old régime was not purely a French phenomenon, there is some weight in such observations. Just so it may be argued that the Russian Revolution of 1917 (which occupies a position of analogous importance in our century) was merely the most dramatic of a whole cluster of similar movements, such as those which – some years before 1917 – finally ended the age-old Turkish and Chinese empires. Yet this is to miss the point. The French Revolution may not have been an isolated phenomenon, but it was far more fundamental than any of the other contemporary ones and its consequences were therefore far more profound. In the first place, it occurred in the most powerful and populous state of Europe (leaving Russia apart). In 1789 something like one European out of every five was a Frenchman. In the second place it was, alone of all the revolutions which preceded and followed it, a mass *social* revolution, and immeasurably more radical than any comparable upheaval. It is no accident that the American revolutionaries, and the British 'Jacobins' who migrated to France because of their political sympathies, found themselves moderates in France. Tom Paine was an extremist in Britain and America; but in Paris he was among the most moderate of the Girondins. The results of the American revolutions were, broadly speaking, countries carrying on much as before, only minus the political control of the British, Spaniards and Portuguese. The result of the French Revolution was that the age of Balzac replaced the age of Mme Dubarry.

In the third place, alone of all the contemporary revolutions, the French was ecumenical. Its armies set out to revolutionize the world; its ideas actually did so. The American revolution has remained a crucial event in American history, but (except for the countries directly involved in and by it) it has left few major traces elsewhere. The French Revolution is a landmark in all countries. Its repercussions rather than those of the American revolution, occasioned the risings which led to the liberation of Latin America after 1808. Its direct influence radiated as far as Bengal, where Ram Mohan Roy was inspired by it to found the first Hindu reform movement and the ancestor of modern Indian nationalism. (When he visited England in 1830, he insisted on travelling in a French ship to demonstrate his enthusiasm for its principles.) It was, as has been well said, 'the first great movement of ideas in Western

Christendom that had any real effect on the world of

Islam',[2] and that almost immediately. By the middle of the nineteenth century the Turkish word 'vatan', hitherto merely describing a man's place of birth or residence, had begun to turn under its influence into something like 'patrie'; the term 'liberty', before 1800 primarily a legal term denoting the opposite to 'slavery', had begun to acquire a new political content. Its indirect influence is universal, for it provided the pattern for all subsequent revolutionary movements, its lessons (interpreted according to taste) being incorporated into modern socialism and communism.[*]

The French Revolution thus remains *the* revolution of its time, and not merely one, though the most prominent, of its kind. And its origins must therefore be sought not merely in the general conditions of Europe, but in the specific situation of France. Its peculiarity is perhaps best illustrated in international terms. Throughout the eighteenth century France was

2 B. Lewis, The Impact of the French Revolution on Turkey, *Journal of World History*, I (1953–4, p. 105).

[*] This is not to underestimate the influence of the American Revolution. It undoubtedly helped to stimulate the French, and in a narrower sense provided constitutional models – in competition and sometimes alternation with the French – for various Latin American states, and inspiration for democratic-radical movements from time to time.

the major international economic rival of Britain. Her foreign trade, which multiplied fourfold between 1720 and 1780, caused anxiety; her colonial system was in certain areas (such as the West Indies) more dynamic than the British. Yet France was not a power like Britain, whose foreign policy was already determined substantially by the interests of capitalist expansion. She was the most powerful and in many ways the most typical of the old aristocratic absolute monarchies of Europe. In other words, the conflict between the official framework and the vested interests of the old régime and the rising new social forces was more acute in France than elsewhere.

The new forces knew fairly precisely what they wanted. Turgot, the physiocrat economist, stood for an efficient exploitation of the land, for free enterprise and trade, for a standardized, efficient administration of a single homogeneous national territory, and the abolition of all restrictions and social inequalities which stood in the way of the development of national resources and rational, equitable administration and taxation. Yet his attempt to apply such a programme as the first minister of Louis XVII in 1774–6 failed lamentably, and the failure is characteristic. Reforms
8   of this character, in modest doses, were not incompat-

ible with or unwelcome to absolute monarchies. On the contrary, since they strengthened their hand, they were, as we have seen, widely propagated at this time among the so-called 'enlightened despots'. But in most of the countries of 'enlightened despotism' such reforms were either inapplicable, and therefore mere theoretical flourishes, or unlikely to change the general character of their political and social structure; or else they failed in the face of the resistance of the local aristocracies and other vested interests, leaving the country to relapse into a somewhat tidied-up version of its former state. In France they failed more rapidly than elsewhere, for the resistance of the vested interests was more effective. But the results of this failure were more catastrophic for the monarchy; and the forces of bourgeois change were far too strong to relapse into inactivity. They merely transformed their hopes from an enlightened monarchy to the people or 'the nation'.

Nevertheless, such a generalisation does not take us far towards an understanding of why the revolution broke out when it did, and why it took the remarkable road it did. For this it is most useful to consider the so-called 'feudal reaction' which actually provided the spark to explode the powder-barrel of France.

The 400,000 or so persons who, among the twenty-three million Frenchmen, formed the nobility, the unquestioned 'first order' of the nation, though not so absolutely safeguarded against the intrusion of lesser orders as in Prussia and elsewhere, were secure enough. They enjoyed considerable privileges, including exemption from several taxes (but not from as many as the better-organized clergy), and the right to receive feudal dues. Politically their situation was less brilliant. Absolute monarchy, while entirely aristocratic and even feudal in its *ethos*, had deprived the nobles of political independence and responsibility and cut down their old representative institutions – estates and *parlements* – so far as possible. The fact continued to rankle among the higher aristocracy and among the more recent *noblesse de robe* created by the kings for various purposes, mostly finance and administration; an ennobled government middle class which expressed the double discontent of aristocrats and bourgeois so far as it could through the surviving law-courts and estates. Economically the nobles' worries were by no means negligible. Fighters rather than earners by birth and tradition – nobles were even formally debarred from exercising a trade or profession – they depended on the income of their estates, or, if they belonged to the favoured minority of large or court nobles, on wealthy marriages, court pensions, gifts and sinecure. But the expenses of noble status were large and rising, their incomes – since they were rarely businesslike managers of their wealth, if they managed it at all – fell. Inflation tended to reduce the value of fixed revenues such as rents.

It was therefore natural that the nobles should use their one main asset, the acknowledged privileges of the order. Throughout the eighteenth century, in France as in many other countries, they encroached steadily upon the official posts which the absolute monarchy had preferred to fill with technically competent and politically harmless middle class men. By the 1780s four quarterings of nobility were needed even to buy a commission in the army, all bishops were nobles and even the keystone of royal administration, the intendancies, had been largely recaptured by them. Consequently the nobility not merely exasperated the feelings of the middle class by their successful competition for official posts; they also undermined the state itself by an increasing tendency to take over provincial and central administration. Similarly they – and especially the poorer provincial gentlemen who had few other resources – attempted to counteract the decline in their income by squeezing the utmost out of their very considerable feudal rights to exact money (or more rarely service) from the peasantry. An entire profession, the *feudists*, came into existence to revive obsolete rights of this kind or to maximize the yield of existing ones. Its most celebrated member, Gracchus Babeuf, was to become the leader of the first communist revolt in modern history in 1796. Consequently the nobility exasperated not only the middle class but also the peasantry.

The position of this vast class, comprising perhaps 80 per cent of all Frenchmen, was far from brilliant. They were indeed in general free, and often landowners. In actual quantity noble estates covered only one-fifth of the land, clerical estates perhaps another 6 per cent with regional variations.[3] Thus in the diocese of Montpellier the peasants already owned 38 to 40 per cent of the land, the bourgeoisie 18 to 19, the nobles 15 to 16, the clergy 3 to 4, while one-fifth was common land.[4] In fact, however, the great majority were landless or with insufficient holdings, a deficiency

3 H. Sée, *Equisse d'une Histoire du Régime Agraire* (1931), pp. 16–17.

4 A. Soboul, *Les Campagnes Montpelliéraines à la fin de l'Ancien Régime* (1958).

increased by the prevailing technical backwardness; and the general land-hunger was intensified by the rise in population. Feudal dues, tithes and taxes took a large and rising proportion of the peasant's income, and inflation reduced the value of the remainder. For only the minority of peasants who had a constant surplus for sale benefited from the rising prices; the rest, in one way or another, suffered from them, especially in times of bad harvest, when famine prices ruled. There is little doubt that in the twenty years preceding the Revolution the situation of the peasants grew worse for these reasons.

The financial troubles of the monarchy brought matters to a head. The administrative and fiscal structure of the kingdom was grossly obsolete, and, as we have seen, the attempt to remedy this by the reforms of 1774–6 failed, defeated by the resistance of vested interests headed by the *parlements*. Then France became involved in the American War of Independence. Victory over England was gained at the cost of final bankruptcy, and thus the American Revolution can claim to be the direct cause of the French. Various expedients were tried with diminishing success, but nothing short of a fundamental reform, which mobilized the real and considerable taxable capacity of the country could cope with a situation in which expenditure outran revenue by at least 20 per cent, and no effective economies were possible. For though the extravagance of Versailles has often been blamed for the crisis, court expenditure only amounted to 6 per cent of the total in 1788. War, navy and diplomacy made up one-quarter, the service of the existing debt one-half. War and debt – the American War and its debt – broke the back of the monarchy.

The government's crisis gave the aristocracy and the *parlements* their chance. They refused to pay without an extension of their privileges. The first breach in the front of absolutism was a hand-picked but nevertheless rebellious 'assembly of notables' called in 1787 to grant the government's demands. The second, and decisive, was the desperate decision to call the States-General – the old feudal assembly of the realm, buried since 1614. The Revolution thus began as an aristocratic attempt to recapture the state. This attempt miscalculated for two reasons: it underestimated the independent intentions of the 'Third Estate' – the fictional entity deemed to represent all who were neither nobles nor clergy, but in fact dominated by the middle class – and it overlooked the profound economic and social crisis into which it threw its political demands.

The French Revolution was not made or led by a formed party or movement in the modern sense, nor by men attempting to carry out a systematic programme. It hardly even threw up 'leaders' of the kind to which twentieth century revolutions have accustomed us, until the post-revolutionary figure of Napoleon. Nevertheless a striking consensus of general ideas among a fairly coherent social group gave the revolutionary movement effective unity. The group was the 'bourgeoisie'; its ideas were those of classical liberalism, as formulated by the 'philosophers' and 'economists' and propagated by freemasonry and in informal associations. To this extent 'the philosophers' can be justly made responsible for the Revolution. It would have occurred without them; but they probably made the difference between a mere breakdown of an old régime and the effective and rapid substitution of a new one.

In its most general form the ideology of 1789 was the masonic one expressed with such innocent sublimity in Mozart's *Magic Flute* (1791), one of the earliest of the great propagandist works of art of an age whose highest artistic achievements so often belonged to propaganda. More specifically, the demands of the *bourgeois* of 1789 are laid down in the famous Declaration of the Rights of Man and Citizens of that year. This document is a manifesto against the hierarchical society of noble privilege, but not one in favour of democratic or egalitarian society. 'Men are born and live free and equal under the laws,' said its first article; but it also provides for the existence of social distinctions, if 'only on grounds of common utility'. Private property was a natural right, sacred, inalienable and inviolable. Men were equal before the law and careers were equally open to talent; but if the race started without handicaps, it was equally assumed that the runners would not finish together. The declaration laid down (as against the noble hierarchy or absolutism) that 'all citizens have a right to co-operate in the formation of the law'; but 'either personally or through their representatives'. And the representative assembly which it envisaged as the fundamental organ of government was not necessarily a democratically elected one, nor the régime it implied one which eliminated kings. A constitutional monarchy based on a propertied oligarchy expressing itself through a representative assembly was more congenial to most bourgeois liberals than the democratic republic which might have seemed a more logical expression of their

theoretical aspirations; though there were some who

did not hesitate to advocate this also. But on the whole the classical liberal bourgeois of 1789 (and the liberal of 1789–1848) was not a democrat but a believer in constitutionalism, a secular state with civil liberties and guarantees for private enterprise, and government by tax-payers and property-owners.

Nevertheless officially such a régime would express not simply his class interests, but the general will of 'the people', which was in turn (a significant identification) 'the French nation'. The king was no longer Louis, by the Grace of God, King of France and Navarre, but Louis, by the Grace of God and the constitutional law of the state, King of the French. 'The source of all sovereignty,' said the Declaration, 'resides essentially in the nation.' And the nation, as Abbé Sieyès put it, recognized no interest on earth above its own, and accepted no law or authority other than its own – neither that of humanity at large nor of other nations. No doubt the French nation, and its subsequent imitators, did not initially conceive of its interests clashing with those of other peoples, but on the contrary saw itself as inaugurating, or taking part in, a movement of the general liberation of peoples from tyranny. But in fact national rivalry (for instance that of French businessmen with British businessmen) 17 and national subordination (for instance that of conquered or liberated nations to the interests of *la grande nation*) were implicit in the nationalism to which the bourgeois of 1789 gave its first official expression. 'The people' identified with 'the nation' was a revolutionary concept; more revolutionary than the bourgeois-liberal programme which purported to express it. But it was also a double-edged one.

Since the peasants and labouring poor were illiterate, politically modest or immature and the process of election indirect, 610 men, mostly of this stamp, were elected to represent the Third Estate. Most were lawyers who played an important economic role in provincial France; about a hundred were capitalists and businessmen. The middle class had fought bitterly and successfully to win a representation as large as that of the nobility and clergy combined, a moderate ambition for a group officially representing 95 per cent of the people. They now fought with equal determination for the right to exploit their potential majority votes by turning thc States General into an assembly of individual deputies voting as such, instead of the traditional feudal body deliberating and voting by 'orders', a situation in which nobility and clergy could always outvote the Third. On this issue the first revolutionary break-through occurred. Some six weeks after the opening of the States General the Commons, anxious to forestall action by king, nobles and clergy, constituted themselves and all who were prepared to join them on their own terms a National Assembly with the right to recast the constitution. An attempt at counter-revolution led them to formulate their claims virtually in terms of the English House of Commons. Absolutism was at an end as Mirabeau, a brilliant and disreputable ex-noble, told the King: 'Sire, you are a stranger in this assembly, you have not the right to speak here.'[5]

The Third Estate succeeded, in the face of the united resistance of the king and the privileged orders, because it represented not merely the views of an educated and militant minority, but of far more powerful forces: the labouring poor of the cities, and especially of Paris, and shortly, also, the revolutionary peasantry. For what turned a limited reform agitation into a revolution was the fact that the calling of the States-General coincided with a profound economic and social crisis. The later 1780s had been, for a complexity of reasons, a period of great difficulties for

5 A. Goodwin, *The French Revolution* (1959 ed.), p. 70.

virtually all branches of the French economy. A bad harvest in 1788 (and 1789) and a very difficult winter made this crisis acute. Bad harvests hurt the peasantry, for while they meant that large producers could sell grain at famine prices, the majority of men on their insufficient holdings might well have to eat up their seed-corn, or buy food at such prices, especially in months immediately preceding the new harvest (i.e. May-July). They obviously hurt the urban poor, whose cost of living – bread was the staple hood – might well double. It hurt them all the more as the impoverishment of the countryside reduced the market for manufactures and therefore also produced an industrial depression. The country poor were therefore desperate and restless with riot and banditry; the urban poor were doubly desperate as work ceased at the very moment that the cost of living soared. Under normal circumstances little more than blind-rioting might have occurred. But in 1788 and 1789 a major convulsion in the kingdom, a campaign of propaganda and election, gave the people's desperation a political perspective. They introduced the tremendous and earth-shaking idea of *liberation* from gentry and oppression. A riotous people stood behind the deputies of the Third

Estate.

Counter-revolution turned a potential mass rising into an actual one. Doubtless it was only natural that the old régime should have fought back, if necessary with armed force; though the army was no longer wholly reliable. (Only unrealistic dreamers can suggest that Louis XVI might have accepted defeat and immediately turned himself into a constitutional monarch, even if he had been a less negligible and stupid man than he was, married to a less chicken-brained and irresponsible woman, and prepared to listen to less disastrous advisers.) In fact counter-revolution mobilized the Paris masses, already hungry, suspicious and militant. The most sensational result of their mobilization was the capture of the Bastille, a state prison symbolizing royal authority, where the revolutionaries expected to find arms. In times of revolution nothing is more powerful than the fall of symbols. The capture of the Bastille, which has rightly made July 14th into the French national day, ratified the fall of despotism and was hailed all over the world as the beginning of liberation. Even the austere philosopher Immanuel Kant of Koenigsberg, it is said, whose habits were so regular that the citizens of that town set their watches by him, postponed the hour of his afternoon stroll when he received the news, thus convincing

Koenigsberg that a world-shaking event had indeed happened. What is more to the point, the fall of the Bastille spread the revolution to the provincial towns and the countryside.

Peasant revolutions are vast, shapeless, anonymous, but irresistible movements. What turned an epidemic of peasant unrest into an irreversible convulsion was a combination of provincial town risings and a wave of mass panic, spreading obscurely but rapidly across vast stretches of the country: the so-called *Grande Peur* of late July and early August 1789. Within three weeks of July 14th the social structure of French rural feudalism and the state machine of royal France lay in fragments. All that remained of state power was a scattering of doubtfully reliable regiments, a National Assembly without coercive force, and a multiplicity of municipal or provincial middle class administrations which soon set up bourgeois armed 'National Guards' on the model of Paris. Middle class and aristocracy immediately accepted the inevitable: all feudal privileges were officially abolished though, when the political situation had settled, a stiff price for their redemption was fixed. Feudalism was not finally abolished until 1793. By the end of August the Revolution had also acquired its formal manifesto, the Declaration of the Rights of Man and Citizen. Conversely, the king resisted with his usual stupidity, and sections of the middle class revolutionaries, frightened by the social implications of the mass upheaval, began to think that the time for conservatism had come.

In brief, the main shape of French and all subsequent bourgeois-revolutionary politics were by now clearly visible. This dramatic dialectical dance was to dominate the future generations. Time and again we shall see moderate middle class reformers mobilizing the masses against die-hard resistance or counter-revolution. We shall see the masses pushing beyond the moderates' aims to their own social revolutions, and the moderates in turn splitting into a conservative group henceforth making common cause with the reactionaries, and a left wing group determined to pursue the rest of the as yet unachieved moderate aims with the help of the masses, even at the risk of losing control over them. And so on through repetitions and variations of the pattern of resistance – mass mobilization – shift to the left – splits among-moderates-and-shift-to-the-right – until either the bulk of the middle class passed into the henceforth conservative camp, or was defeated by social revolution. In most subsequent bourgeois revolutions the moderate 23 liberals were to pull back, or transfer into the conservative camp, at a very early stage. Indeed in the nineteenth century we increasingly find (most notably in Germany) that they became unwilling to begin revolution at all, for fear of its incalculable consequences, preferring a compromise with king and aristocracy. The peculiarity of the French Revolution is that one section of the liberal middle class was prepared to remain revolutionary up to and indeed beyond the brink of anti-bourgeois revolution: these were the Jacobins, whose name came to stand for 'radical revolution' everywhere.

Why? Partly, of course, because the French bourgeoisie had not yet, like subsequent liberals, the awful memory of the French Revolution to be frightened of. After 1794 it would be clear to moderates that the Jacobin régime had driven the Revolution too far for bourgeois comfort and prospects, just as it would be clear to revolutionaries that 'the sun of 1793', if it were to rise again, would have to shine on a non-bourgeois society. Again, the Jacobins could afford radicalism because in their time no class existed which could provide a coherent social alternative to theirs. Such a class only arose in the course of the industrial revolution, with the 'proletariat' or, more precisely, with the ideologies and movements based on it. In the French Revolution the working class – and even this is a misnomer for the aggregate of hired, but mostly nonindustrial, wage-earners – as yet played no significant independent part. They hungered, they rioted, perhaps they dreamed; but for practical purposes they followed non-proletarian leaders. The peasantry never provides a political alternative to anyone; merely, as occasion dictates, an almost irresistible force or an almost immovable object. The only alternative to bourgeois radicalism (if we except small bodies of ideologues or militants powerless when deprived of mass support) were the 'Sansculottes', a shapeless, mostly urban movement of the labouring poor, small craftsmen, shopkeepers, artisans, tiny entrepreneurs and the like. The Sansculottes were organized, notably in the 'sections' of Paris and the local political clubs, and provided the main striking-force of the revolution – the actual demonstrators, rioters, constructors of barricades. Through journalists like Marat and Hébert, through local spokesmen, they also formulated a policy, behind which lay a vaguely defined and contradictory social ideal, combining respect for (small) private property with hostility to the rich, government-guaranteed work, wages and social security for the poor man, an extreme, egalitarian and libertarian democracy, localized and direct. In fact the Sansculottes were one branch of that universal and important political trend which sought to express the interests of the great mass of 'little men' who existed between the poles of the 'bourgeois' and the 'proletarian', often perhaps rather nearer the latter than the former because they were, after all, mostly poor. We can observe it in the United States (as Jeffersonianism and Jacksonian democracy, or populism), in Britain (as 'radicalism'), in France (as the ancestors of the future 'republicans' and radical-socialists), in Italy (as Mazzinians and Garibaldians), and elsewhere. Mostly it tended to settle down, in postrevolutionary ages, as a left-wing of middle-class liberalism, but one loth to abandon the ancient principle that there are no enemies on the left, and ready, in times of crisis, to rebel against 'the wall of money' or 'the economic royalists' or 'the cross of gold crucifying mankind'. But Sansculottism provided no real alternative either. Its ideal, a golden past of villagers and small craftsmen or a golden future of small farmers and artisans undisturbed by bankers and millionaires, was unrealizable. History moved dead against them. The most

they could do – and this they achieved in 1793–4 –

was to erect roadblocks in its path, which have hampered French economic growth from that day almost to this. In fact Sansculottism was so helpless a phenomenon that its very name is largely forgotten, or remembered only as a synonym of Jacobinism, which provided it with leadership in the year II.

II

Between 1789 and 1791 the victorious moderate bourgeoisie, acting through what had now become the Constituent Assembly, set about the gigantic rationalization and reform of France which was its object. Most of the lasting institutional achievements of the Revolution date from this period, as do its most striking international results, the metric system and the pioneer emancipation of the Jews. Economically the perspectives of the Constituent Assembly were entirely liberal: its policy for the peasantry was the enclosure of common lands and the encouragement of rural entrepreneurs, for the working-class, the banning of trade unions, for the small crafts, the abolition of guilds and corporations. It gave little concrete satisfaction to the common people, except, from 1790, by means of the secularization and sale of church lands (as well as those of the emigrant nobility) which had 28 the triple advantage of weakening clericalism, strengthening the provincial and peasant entrepreneur, and giving many peasants a measurable return for their revolutionary activity. The Constitution of 1791 fended off excessive democracy by a system of constitutional monarchy based on an admittedly rather wide property-franchise of 'active citizens'. The passive, it was hoped, would live up to their name.

In fact, this did not happen. On the one hand the monarchy, though now strongly supported by a powerful ex-revolutionary bourgeois faction, could not resign itself to the new regime. The Court dreamed of and intrigued for a crusade of royal cousins to expel the governing rabble of commoners and restore God's anointed, the most Catholic king of France, to his rightful place. The Civil Constitution of the Clergy (1790), a misconceived attempt to destroy, not the Church, but the Roman absolutist allegiance of the Church, drove the majority of the clergy and of their faithful into opposition, and helped to drive the king into the desperate, and as it proved suicidal, attempt to flee the country. He was recaptured at Varennes (June 1791) and henceforth republicanism became a mass force; for traditional kings who abandon their peoples lose the right to loyalty. On the other hand, the uncontrolled free enterprise economy of the moderates accentuated the fluctuations in the level of food-prices, and consequently the militancy of the urban poor, especially in Paris. The price of bread registered the political temperature of Paris with the accuracy of a thermometer; and the Paris masses were the decisive revolutionary force: not for nothing was the new French tricolour constructed by combining the old royal white with the red-and-blue colours of Paris.

The outbreak of war brought matters to a head; that is to say it led to the second revolution of 1792, the Jacobin Republic of the Year II, and eventually to Napoleon. In other words it turned the history of the French Revolution into the history of Europe.

Two forces pushed France into a general war: the extreme right and the moderate left. For the king, the French nobility and the growing aristocratic and ecclesiastical emigration, camped in various West German cities, it was evident that only foreign intervention could restore the old regime.* Such intervention was not too easily organized, given the complexities of the international situation, and the relative political tranquillity of other countries. However, it was

---

* Something like 300,000 Frenchmen emigrated between 1789
and 1795.[6]

increasingly evident to nobles and divinely appointed rulers elsewhere that the restoration of Louis XVI's power was not merely an act of class solidarity, but an important safeguard against the spread of the appalling ideas propagated from France. Consequently the forces for the reconquest of France gathered abroad.

At the same time the moderate liberals themselves, most notably the group of politicians clustering round the deputies from the mercantile Gironde department, were a bellicose force. This was partly because every genuine revolution tends to be ecumenical. For Frenchmen, as for their numerous sympathisers abroad, the liberation of France was merely the first instalment of the universal triumph of liberty; an attitude which led easily to the conviction that it was the duty of the fatherland of revolution to liberate all peoples groaning under oppression and tyranny. There was a genuinely exalted and generous passion to spread freedom among the revolutionaries, moderate and extreme; a genuine inability to separate the cause of the French nation from that of all enslaved humanity. Both the

6 C. Bloch, L'émigration francaise au XIX siècle, *Etudes d'Histoire Moderne & Contemp.* I (1947), p. 137; D. Greer, *The Incidence of the Emigration during the French Revolution* (1951) however, suggests a very much smaller figure.

French and all other revolutionary movements were to accept this view, or to adapt it, henceforth until at least 1848. All plans for European liberation until 1848 hinged on a joint rising of peoples under the leadership of the French to overthrow European reaction; and after 1830 other movements of national and liberal revolt, such as the Italian or Polish, also tended to see their own nations in some sense as Messiahs destined by their own freedom to initiate everyone else's.

On the other hand, considered less idealistically, war would also help to solve numerous domestic problems. It was tempting and obvious to ascribe the difficulties of the new régime to the plots of emigrés and foreign tyrants, and to divert popular discontents against these. More specifically, businessmen argued that the uncertain economic prospects, the devaluation of the currency and other troubles could only be remedied if the threat of intervention were dispersed. They and their ideologist might reflect, with a glance at the record of Britain, that economic supremacy was the child of systematic aggressiveness. (The eighteenth century was not one in which the successful businessman was at all wedded to peace.) Moreover, as was soon to appear, war could be made to produce profit.

For all these reasons the majority of the new Legislative Assembly, except for a small right wing and a small left wing under Robespierre, preached war. For these reasons also, when war came, the conquests of the revolution were to combine liberation, exploitation and political diversion.

War was declared in April 1792. Defeat, which the people (plausibly enough) ascribed to royal sabotage and treason, brought radicalization. In August-September the monarchy was overthrown, the Republic one and indivisible established, a new age in human history proclaimed with the institution of the Year I of the revolutionary calendar, by the armed action of the Sansculotte masses of Paris. The iron and heroic age of the French Revolution began among the massacres of the political prisoners, the elections to the National Convention – probably the most remarkable assembly in the history of parliamentarism – and the call for total resistance to the invaders. The king was imprisoned, the foreign invasion halted by an undramatic artillery duel at Valmy.

Revolutionary wars impose their own logic. The dominant party in the new Convention were the Girondins, bellicose abroad and moderate at home, a body of parliamentary orators of charm and brilliance representing big business, the provincial bourgeoisie and much intellectual distinction. Their policy was utterly impossible. For only states waging limited campaigns with established regular forces could hope to keep war and domestic affairs in watertight compartments, as the ladies and gentlemen in Jane Austen's novels were just then doing in Britain. The Revolution waged neither a limited campaign nor had it established forces: for its war oscillated between the maximum victory of world revolution and the maximum defeat which meant total counter-revolution, and its army – what was left of the old French army – was ineffective and unreliable. Dumouriez, the Republic's leading general, was shortly to desert to the enemy. Only unprecedented and revolutionary methods could win in such a war, even if victory were to mean merely the defeat of foreign intervention. In fact, such methods were found. In the course of its crisis the young French Republic discovered or invented total war: the total mobilization of a nation's resources through conscription, rationing and a rigidly controlled war economy, and virtual abolition, at home or abroad, of the distinction between soldiers and civilians. How appalling the implications of this discovery are has only become clear in our own historic epoch. Since the revolutionary war of 1792–4 remained an exceptional episode, most nineteenth-century observers could make no sense of it, except to observe (until in the fatness of later Victorian times even this was forgotten) that wars lead to revolutions, and revolutions win otherwise unwinnable wars. Only today can we see how much about the Jacobin Republic and the 'Terror' of 1793–4 makes sense in no other terms than those of a modern total war effort.

The Sansculottes welcomed a revolutionary war government, not only because they rightly argued that counter-revolution and foreign intervention could only thus be defeated, but also because its methods mobilized the people and brought social justice nearer. (They overlooked the fact that no effective modern war effort is compatible with the decentralized voluntarist direct democracy which they cherished.) The Gironde, on the other hand, was afraid of the political consequences of the combination of mass revolution and war which they unleashed. Nor were they equipped for competition with the left. They did not want to try or execute the king, but had to compete with their rivals, 'the Mountain' (the Jacobins), for this symbol of revolutionary zeal; the Mountain gained prestige, not they. On the other hand, they did want to extend the war into a general ideological crusade of liberation and a direct challenge to the great economic rival, Britain. They succeeded in this object. By March 1793 France was at war with most of Europe, and had begun foreign annexations (legitimized by the newly-invented doctrine of France's right to her 'natural frontiers'). But the expansion of the war, all the more as it went badly, only strengthened the hands of the left, which alone could win it. Retreating and outmanoeuvred, the Gironde was finally driven to ill-judged attacks against the left, which were soon to turn into organized provincial revolt against Paris. A rapid coup by the Sansculottes overthrew it on June 2, 1793. The Jacobin Republic had come.

III

When the educated layman thinks of the French Revolution it is the events of 1789 but especially the Jacobin Republic of the Year II which chiefly come to his mind. The prim Robespierre, the huge and whoring Danton, the icy revolutionary elegance of Saint-Just, the gross Marat, committee of public safety, revolutionary tribunal and guillotine are the images which we see most clearly. The very names of the moderate revolutionaries who come between Mirabeau and Lafayette in 1789 and the Jacobin leaders in 1793, have lapsed from all but the memory of historians. The Girondins are remembered only as a group, and perhaps for the politically negligible but romantic women attached to them – Mme Roland or Charlotte Corday. Who, outside the expert field, knows even the names of Brissot, Vergniaud, Guadet and the rest? Conservatives have created a lasting image of The Terror, dictatorship and hysterical bloodlust unchained, though by twentieth century standards, and indeed by the standards of conservative repressions of social revolution such as the massacres after the Paris Commune of 1871, its mass killings were relatively modest, 17,000 official executions in fourteen months.[7] Revolutionaries, especially in France, have seen it as the first people's republic, the inspiration of all subsequent revolt. For all it was an era not to be measured by everyday human criteria.

That is true. But for the solid middle class Frenchman who stood behind The Terror, it was neither pathological nor apocalyptic, but first and foremost the only effective method of preserving their country. This the Jacobin Republic did, and its achievement was superhuman. In June 1793 sixty out of the eighty departments of France were in revolt against Paris; the armies of the German princes were invading France from the north and east; the British attacked from the south and west: the country was helpless and bankrupt. Fourteen months later all France was under firm control, the invaders had been expelled, the French armies in turn occupied Belgium and were about to enter on twenty years of almost unbroken and effort-

7 D. Greer, *The Incidence of the Terror* (Harvard 1935).

less military triumph. Yet by March 1794 an army three times as large as before was run at half the cost of March 1793, and the value of the French currency (or rather of the paper *assignats* which had largely replaced it) was kept approximately stable, in marked contrast to both past and future. No wonder Jeanbon St André, the Jacobin member of the Committee of Public Safety who, though a firm republican, later became one of Napoleon's most efficient prefects, looked at imperial France with contempt as it staggered under the defeats of 1812–3. The Republic of the Year II had coped with worse crises, and with fewer resources.*

For such men, as indeed for the majority of the National Convention which at bottom retained control throughout this heroic period, the choice was simple: either The Terror with all its defects from the middle class point of view, or the destruction of the

* 'Do you know what kind of government (was victorious)? . . . A government of the Convention. A government of passionate Jacobins in red bonnets, wearing rough woollen cloth, wooden shoes, who lived on simple bread and bad beer and went to sleep on mattresses laid on the floor of their meeting-halls, when they were too tired to wake and deliberate further. That is the kind of men who saved France. I was one of them, gentlemen. And here, as in the apartments of the Emperor which I am about to enter, I glory in the fact.' Quoted J. Savant, *Les Prefets de Napoléon* (1958), 111–12.

Revolution, the disintegration of the national state, and probably – was there not the example of Poland? – the disappearance of the country. Very likely, but for the desperate crisis of France, many among them would have preferred a less iron régime and certainly a less firmly controlled economy: the fall of Robespierre led to an epidemic of economic decontrol and corrupt racketeering which, incidentally, culminated in galloping inflation and the national bankruptcy of 1797. But even from the narrowest point of view, the prospects of the French middle class depended on those of a unified strong centralized national state. And anyway, could the Revolution which had virtually created the term 'nation' and 'patriotism' in their modern senses, abandon the *grande nation*?

The first task of the Jacobin régime was to mobilize mass support against the dissidence of the Gironde and the provincial notables, and to retain the already mobilized mass support of the Paris Sansculottes, some of whose demands for a revolutionary war-effort – general conscription (the 'levée en masse'), terror against the 'traitors' and general price-control (the 'maximum') – in any case coincided with Jacobin common sense, though their other demands were to

prove troublesome. A somewhat radicalized new constitution, hitherto delayed by the Gironde, was proclaimed. According to this noble but academic document the people were offered universal suffrage, the right of insurrection, work or maintenance, and – most significant of all – the official statement that the happiness of all was the aim of government and the people's rights were to be not merely available but operative. It was the first genuinely democratic constitution proclaimed by a modern state. More concretely, the Jacobins abolished all remaining feudal rights without indemnity, improved the small buyer's chance to purchase the forfeited land of emigrés, and – some months later – abolished slavery in the French colonies, in order to encourage the Negroes of San Domingo to fight for the Republic against the English. These measures had the most far-reaching results. In America they helped to create the first independent revolutionary leader of stature in Toussaint-Louverture.* In France they established that impregnable citadel of small and middle peasant proprietors, small

---

* The failure of Napoleonic France to recapture Haiti was one of the main reasons for liquidating the entire remaining American Empire, which was sold by the Louisiana Purchase (1803) to the USA. Thus a further consequence of spreading Jacobinism to America was to make the USA a continent-wide power.

craftsmen and shopkeepers, economically retrogressive but passionately devoted to Revolution and Republic, which has dominated the country's life ever since. The capitalist transformation of agriculture and small enterprise, the essential condition for rapid economic development, was slowed to a crawl; and with it the speed of urbanization, the expansion of the home market, the multiplication of the working-class and, incidentally, the ulterior advance of proletarian revolution. Both big business and the labour movement were long doomed to remain minority phenomena in France, islands surrounded by a sea of corner grocers, peasant smallholders and café proprietors.

The centre of the new government, representing as it did an alliance of Jacobin and Sansculotte, therefore shifted perceptibly to the left. This was reflected in the reconstructed Committee of Public Safety, which rapidly became the effective war-cabinet of France. It lost Danton, a powerful, dissolute, probably corrupt, but immensely talented revolutionary more moderate than he looked (he had been a minister in the last royal administration) and gained Maximilien Robespierre, who became its most influential member. Few historians have been dispassionate about this dandyish, thin-blooded, fanatical lawyer with his somewhat excessive sense of private monopoly in virtue, because he still incarnates the terrible and glorious year II about which no man is neutral. He was not an agreeable individual; even those who think he was right nowadays tend to prefer the shining mathematical rigour of that architect of Spartan paradises, the young Saint-Just. He was not a great man and often a narrow one. But he is the only individual thrown up by the Revolution (other than Napoleon) about whom a cult has grown up. This is because for him, as for history, the Jacobin Republic was not a war-winning device but an ideal: the terrible and glorious reign of justice and virtue when all good citizens were equal in the sight of the nation and the people smote the traitors. Jean-Jacques Rousseau and the crystalline conviction of rightness gave him his strength. He had no formal dictatorial powers or even office, being merely one member of the Committee of Public Safety, which was in turn merely one sub-committee – the most powerful, though never all-powerful – of the Convention. His power was that of the people – the Paris masses; his terror theirs. When they abandoned him he fell.

The tragedy of Robespierre and the Jacobin Republic was that they were themselves obliged to alienate this support. The régime was an alliance between middle class and labouring masses; but for the middle class Jacobins, Sansculotte concessions were tolerable only because, and as far as, they attached the masses to the régime without terrifying property-owners; and within the alliance the middle class Jacobins were decisive. Moreover, the very needs of the war obliged any government to centralize and discipline, at the expense of the free, local, direct democracy of club and section, the casual voluntarist militia, the free argumentative elections on which the Sansculottes thrived. The process which, during the Spanish Civil War of 1936–9, strengthened Communists at the expense of Anarchists, strengthened Jacobins of Saint Just's stamp at the expense of Sansculottes of Hébert's. By 1794 government and politics were monolithic and run in harness by direct agents of Committee or Convention – through delegates *en mission* – and a large body of Jacobin officers and officials in conjunction with local party organizations. Lastly, the economic needs of the war alienated popular support. In the towns price-control and rationing benefited the masses; but the corresponding wage-freeze hurt them. In the countryside the systematic requisitioning of food (which the urban Sansculottes had been the first to advocate) alienated the peasantry.

The masses therefore retired into discontent or into a puzzled and resentful passivity, especially after the trial and execution of the Hébertists, the most vocal spokesmen of the Sansculotterie. Meanwhile more moderate supporters were alarmed by the attack on the right wing opposition, now headed by Danton. This faction had provided a refuge for numerous racketeers, speculators, black market operators and other corrupt though capital-accumulating elements, all the more readily as Danton himself embodied the a-moral, Falstaffian, free loving and free spending which always emerges initially in social revolutions until overpowered by the hard puritanism that invariably comes to dominate them. The Dantons of history are always defeated by the Robespierres (or by those who pretend to behave like Robespierres) because hard narrow dedication can succeed where bohemianism cannot. However, if Robespierre won moderate support for eliminating corruption, which was after all in the interests of the war-effort, the further restrictions on freedom and money-making were more disconcerting to the businessman. Finally, no large body of opinion liked the somewhat fanciful ideological excursions of the period – the systematic dechristianization campaigns (due to Sansculotte zeal) and Robespierre's new civic religion of the Supreme Being, complete with ceremonies, which attempted to counteract the atheists and carry out the precepts of the divine Jean-Jacques. And the steady hiss of the guillotine reminded all politicians that no one was really safe.

By April 1794, both right and left had gone to the guillotine and the Robespierrists were therefore politically isolated. Only the war-crisis maintained them in power. When, late in June 1794, the new armies of the Republic proved their firmness by decisively defeating the Austrians at Fleurus and occupying Belgium, the end was at hand. On the Ninth Thermidor by the revolutionary calender (July 27, 1794) the Convention overthrew Robespierre. The next day he, Saint-Just and Couthon were executed, and so a few days later were eighty-seven members of the revolutionary Paris Commune.

IV

Thermidor is the end of the heroic and remembered phase of the Revolution: the phase of ragged Sansculottes and correct red-bonneted citizens who saw themselves as Brutus and Cato, of the grandiloquent classical and generous, but also of the mortal phrases: 'Lyon n'est plus', 'Ten thousand soldiers lack shoes. You will take the shoes of all the aristocrats in Strasbourg and deliver them ready for transport to headquarters by tomorrow ten a.m.'[8] It was not a comfortable phase to live through, for most men were hungry and many afraid; but it was a phenomenon as awful and irreversible as the first nuclear explosion, and all history has been permanently changed by it. And the energy it generated was sufficient to sweep away the armies of the old régimes of Europe like straw.

8 *Oeuvres Complètes de Saint-Just*, Vol. II, p. 147 (ed. C. Vellay, Paris 1908).

The problem which faced the French middle class for the remainder of what is technically described as the revolutionary period (1794–9) was how to achieve political stability and economic advance on the basis of the original liberal programme of 1789–91. It has never solved this problem adequately from that day to this, though from 1870 on it was to discover a workable formula for most times in the parliamentary republic. The rapid alternations of régime – Directory (1795–9), Consulate (1799–1804), Empire (1804–14), restored Bourbon Monarchy (1815–30), Constitutional Monarchy (1830–48), Republic (1848–51), and Empire (1852–70) – were all attempts to maintain a bourgeois society while avoiding the double danger of the Jacobin democratic republic and the old régime.

The great weakness of the Thermidorians was that they enjoyed no political support but at most toleration, squeezed as they were between a revived aristocratic reaction and the Jacobin-Sansculotte Paris poor who soon regretted the fall of Robespierre. In 1795 they devised an elaborate constitution of checks and balances to safeguard themselves against both, and periodic shifts to right and left maintained them precariously in balance; but increasingly they had to rely on the army to disperse the opposition. It was a situation curiously similar to the Fourth Republic, and its conclusion was similar: the rule of a general. But the Directory depended on the army for more than the suppression of periodic coups and plots (various ones in 1795, Babeuf's conspiracy in 1796, Fructidor in 1797, Floréal in 1798, Prairial in 1799).* Inactivity was the only safe guarantee of power for a weak and unpopular régime, but initiative and expansion was what the middle class needed. The army solved this apparently insoluble problem. It conquered; it paid for itself; more than this, its loot and conquests paid for the government. Was it surprising that eventually the most intelligent and able of the army leaders, Napoleon Bonaparte, should have decided that the army could dispense altogether with the feeble civilian régime?

This revolutionary army was the most formidable child of the Jacobin Republic. From a 'levée en masse' of revolutionary citizens it soon turned into a force of professional fighters, for there was no call-up between 1793 and 1798, and those who had no taste or talent for soldiering deserted en masse. It therefore retained

---

* The names are those of months in the revolutionary calendar.

the characteristics of the Revolution and acquired those of the vested interest; the typical Bonapartist mixture. The Revolution gave it its unprecedented military superiority, which Napoleon's superb generalship was to exploit. It always remained something of an improvised levy, in which barely trained recruits picked up training and morale from old sweats, formal barrack-discipline was negligible, soldiers were treated as men and the absolute rule of promotion by merit (which meant distinction in battle) produced a simple hierarchy of courage. This and the sense of arrogant revolutionary mission made the French army independent of the resources on which more orthodox forces depended. It never acquired an effective supply system, for it lived off the country. It was never backed by an armaments industry faintly adequate to its nominal needs; but it won its battles so quickly that it needed few arms: in 1806 the great machine of the Prussian army crumbled before an army in which an entire corps fired a mere 1,400 cannon shot. Generals could rely on unlimited offensive courage and a fair amount of local initiative. Admittedly it also had the weakness of its origins. Apart from Napoleon and a very few others, its generalship and staff-work was poor, for

the revolutionary general or Napoleonic marshal was

most likely a tough sergeant-major or company-officer type promoted for bravery and leadership rather than brains: the heroic but very stupid Marshal Ney was only too typical. Napoleon won battles; his marshals alone tended to lose them. Its sketchy supply system sufficed in the rich and lootable countries where it had been developed: Belgium, North Italy, Germany. In the waste spaces of Poland and Russia, as we shall see, it collapsed. Its total absence of sanitary services multiplied casualties: between 1800 and 1815 Napoleon lost 40 per cent of his forces (though about one-third of this through desertion); but between 90 and 98 per cent of these losses were men who died not in battle but of wounds, sickness, exhaustion and cold. In brief, it was an army which conquered all Europe in short sharp bursts not only because it could, but because it had to.

On the other hand the army was a career like any other of the many the bourgeois revolution had opened to talent; and those who succeeded in it had a vested interest in internal stability like any other bourgeois. That is what made the army, in spite of its built-in Jacobinism, a pillar of the post-Thermidorian government, and its leader Bonaparte a suitable person to conclude the bourgeois revolution and begin the bour- 51 geois régime. Napoleon Bonaparte himself, though of gentlemanly birth by the standards of his barbarous island-home of Corsica, was himself a typical careerist of this kind. Born in 1769 he made his way slowly in the artillery, one of the few branches of the royal army in which technical competence was indispensable, ambitious, discontented and revolutionary. Under the Revolution, and especially under the Jacobin dictatorship which he supported strongly, he was recognized by a local commissar on a crucial front – a fellow Corsican incidentally, which can hardly have harmed his prospects – as a soldier of splendid gifts and promise. The Year II made him a general. He survived the fall of Robespierre, and a gift for cultivating useful connections in Paris helped him forward after this difficult moment. He seized his opportunities in the Italian campaign of 1796 which made him the unchallenged first soldier of the Republic, who acted virtually in independence of the civilian authorities. Power was half-thrust upon him, half grasped by him when the foreign invasions of 1799 revealed the Directory's feebleness and his own indispensability. He became First Consul; then Consul for life; then Emperor. And with his arrival, as by a miracle, the insoluble problems of the Directory became soluble. Within a few years

France had a Civil Code, a concordat with the Church and even, most striking symbol of bourgeois stability, a National Bank. And the world had its first secular myth.

Older readers or those in old-fashioned countries will know the Napoleonic myth as it existed throughout the century when no middle-class cabinet was complete without his busts and pamphleteering wits could argue, even for a joke, that he was not a man but a sun-god. The extraordinary power of this myth can be adequately explained neither by Napoleonic victories nor by Napoleonic propaganda, nor even by Napoleon's own undoubted genius. As a man he was unquestionably very brilliant, versatile, intelligent and imaginative, though power made him rather nasty. As a general he had no equal; as a ruler he was a superbly efficient planner, chief and executive and sufficient of an all-round intellectual to understand and supervise what his subordinates were doing. As an individual he appears to have radiated a sense of greatness; but most of those who testify to this – like Goethe – saw him at the peak of his fame, when the myth already enveloped him. He was, without any question, a very great man, and – perhaps with the exception of Lenin – his picture is the one which most reasonably educated men would, even today, recognize most readily in the portrait gallery of history, if only by the triple trade-mark of the small size, the hair brushed forward over the forehead and the hand pushed into the half-open waistcoat. It is perhaps pointless to measure him against twentieth-century candidates for greatness.

For the Napoleonic myth is based less on Napoleon's merits than on the facts, then unique, of his career. The great known world-shakers of the past had begun as kings like Alexander or patricians like Julius Caesar; but Napoleon was the 'little corporal' who rose to rule a continent by sheer personal talent. (This was not strictly true, but his rise was sufficiently meteoric and high to make the description reasonable.) Every young intellectual who devoured books, as the young Bonaparte had done, wrote bad poems and novels, and adored Rousseau could henceforth see the sky as his limit, laurels surrounding his monogram. Every businessman henceforth had a name for his ambition: to be – the clichés themselves say so – a 'Napoleon of finance' or industry. All common men were thrilled by the sight, then unique, of a common man who became greater than those born to wear crowns. Napoleon gave ambition a personal name at the moment when the double revolution had opened the world to men of ambition. Yet he was more. He was the civilized man of the eighteenth century, rationalist, inquisitive, enlightened, but with sufficient of the disciple of Rousseau about him to be also the romantic man of the nineteenth. He was the man of the Revolution, and the man who brought stability. In a word, he was the figure every man who broke with tradition could identify himself with in his dreams.

For the French he was also something much simpler: the most successful ruler in their long history. He triumphed gloriously abroad; but at home he also established or re-established the apparatus of French institutions as they exist to this day. Admittedly most – perhaps all – his ideas were anticipated by Revolution and Directory; his personal contribution was to make them rather more conservative, hierarchical and authoritarian. But his predecessors anticipated: he carried out. The great lucid monuments of French law, the Codes which became models for the entire non-Anglo-Saxon bourgeois world, were Napoleonic. The hierarchy of officials, from the prefects down, of courts, of university and schools, was his. The great 'careers' of French public life, army, civil service, education, law still have their Napoleonic shapes. He brought stability and prosperity to all except the quarter-of-a-million Frenchmen who did not return from his wars; and even to their relatives he brought glory. No doubt the British saw themselves fighting for liberty against tyranny; but in 1815 most Englishmen were probably poorer and worse off than they had been in 1800, while most Frenchmen were almost certainly better off; nor had any except the still negligible wage-labourers lost the substantial economic benefits of the Revolution. There is little mystery about the persistence of Bonapartism as an ideology of non-political Frenchmen, especially the richer peasantry, after his fall. It took a second and smaller Napoleon to dissipate it between 1851 and 1870.

He had destroyed only one thing: the Jacobin Revolution, the dream of equality, liberty and fraternity, and of the people rising in its majesty to shake off oppression. It was a more powerful myth than his, for after his fall it was this, and not his memory, which inspired the revolutions of the nineteenth century, even in his own country.

Phoenix 60p Paperbacks

History/Biography/Travel
The Empire of Rome A.D. 98–190 *Edward Gibbon*
The Prince *Machiavelli*
The Alan Clark Diaries: Thatcher's Fall *Alan Clark*
Churchill: Embattled Hero *Andrew Roberts*
The French Revolution *E.J. Hobsbawm*
Voyage Around the Horn *Joshua Slocum*
The Great Fire of London *Samuel Pepys*
Utopia *Thomas More*
The Holocaust *Paul Johnson*
Tolstoy and History *Isaiah Berlin*

Science and Philosophy
A Guide to Happiness *Epicurus*
Natural Selection *Charles Darwin*
Science, Mind & Cosmos *John Brockman, ed.*
Zarathustra *Friedrich Nietzsche*
God's Utility Function *Richard Dawkins*
Human Origins *Richard Leakey*
Sophie's World: The Greek Philosophers *Jostein Gaarder*
The Rights of Woman *Mary Wollstonecraft*
The Communist Manifesto *Karl Marx & Friedrich Engels*
Birds of Heaven *Ben Okri*

Fiction
Riot at Misri Mandi *Vikram Seth*
The Time Machine *H. G. Wells*

Love in the Night *F. Scott Fitzgerald*
The Murders in the Rue Morgue *Edgar Allan Poe*
The Necklace *Guy de Maupassant*
You Touched Me *D. H. Lawrence*
The Mabinogion *Anon*
Mowgli's Brothers *Rudyard Kipling*
Shancarrig *Maeve Binchy*
A Voyage to Lilliput *Jonathan Swift*

POETRY
Songs of Innocence and Experience *William Blake*
The Eve of Saint Agnes *John Keats*
High Waving Heather *The Brontes*
Sailing to Byzantium *W. B. Yeats*
I Sing the Body Electric *Walt Whitman*
The Ancient Mariner *Samuel Taylor Coleridge*
Intimations of Immortality *William Wordsworth*
Palgrave's Golden Treasury of Love Poems *Francis Palgrave*
Goblin Market *Christina Rossetti*
Fern Hill *Dylan Thomas*

LITERATURE OF PASSION
Don Juan *Lord Byron*
From Bed to Bed *Catullus*
Satyricon *Petronius*
Love Poems *John Donne*
Portrait of a Marriage *Nigel Nicolson*
The Ballad of Reading Gaol *Oscar Wilde*
Love Sonnets *William Shakespeare*
Fanny Hill *John Cleland*
The Sexual Labyrinth (for women) *Alina Reyes*
Close Encounters (for men) *Alina Reyes*